A YEAR IN THE
City

by Sally Hewitt
Photographs by Chris Fairclough

W
FRANKLIN WATTS
LONDON•SYDNEY

This edition 2008
First published in 2004 by Franklin Watts
338 Euston Road, London NW1 3BH

Franklin Watts Australia
Level 17/207 Kent Street, Sydney NSW 2000

© Franklin Watts 2004

Editor: Kate Newport
Art director: Jonathan Hair
Designer: Steve Prosser

Photographs:
Rob Bowden: 26.
All other photography by Chris Fairclough.

A CIP catalogue record for this book
is available from the British Library

ISBN 978 0 7496 8307 8

Printed in Malaysia

Franklin Watts is a division of Hachette
Children's Books, an Hachette Livre UK company.

CONTENTS

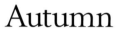

Spring

It is Spring in the city.
The trees grow fresh
green leaves.

Pavement cafés put out
their tables and chairs.

Spring brings sunshine
and showers.

Shoppers need their
umbrellas in the rain.

Birds live in the city, too.

It is easy for them to find
food in the Spring.

The park is full of Spring flowers.

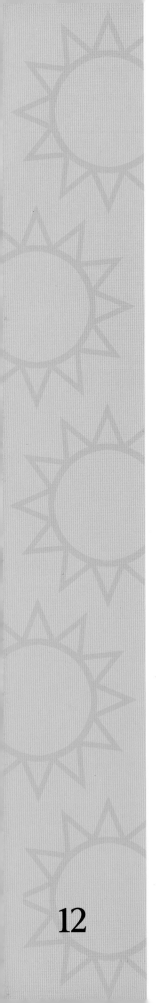

Summer

In Summer, you can eat lunch on the city pavements.

You may hear the sound
of the ice-cream van.

An ice-cream helps you
cool down.

It is hot on the city streets.

The trees give shade.

City workers take off their jackets and coats.

In the park, people
escape from the
noise and heat of
the city.

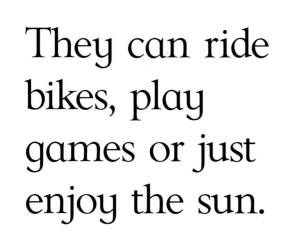

They can ride
bikes, play
games or just
enjoy the sun.

Autumn

In Autumn, the leaves change colour and fall to the ground.

They have to be cleared away from the city streets and parks.

Headlights shine through the early morning mist.

You need to dress up
warmly to sit outside.

In the park, huge bonfires
are built for bonfire night.

Fireworks bang and crackle
and light up the sky.

Pets must be kept safely
indoors.

Winter

In Winter, branches on the city trees are bare.

People get cold waiting at
bus stops.

The newspaper seller
gets cold, being
outside all day.

In the cold weather there is less food for the birds.

A Christmas tree means
that the holidays
are coming.

Lights in shop windows
brighten up the dark
winter streets.

INDEX